Dave Granlund

Editorial Cartoonist

Pulling It All Together

The METROWEST
DAILY NEWS

COMMUNITY
NEWSPAPER
COMPANY
A Herald Media Company

Copyright© 2005   •   ISBN: 1-59725-025-2

Published by Pediment Publishing, a division of The Pediment Group, Inc. www.pediment.com Printed in Canada

For my wife,
Shirley

Acknowledgments

I wish to thank Patrick J. Purcell, Publisher of Herald Media Inc., and Gregory R. Rush, Associate Publisher and Chief Operations Officer of Community Newspaper Company for making this book happen. I wish to also thank Al Getler, Vice President of Circulation for Community Newspaper Company for intitiating this project.

In addition, I offer my sincere gratitude to my readers for allowing me to be part of their daily lives throughout the years.

Lastly, my deep appreciation to my wife and children for their continued creative input, inspiration and valued critiques.

— Dave Granlund

Foreword

On the wall of my office in Washington, I have a cartoon that Dave Granlund drew a few years ago at the time of my birthday. In it, I'm barreling past a reporter asking me if I'm going to slow down after turning 70. I love this cartoon. But it could easily be Dave himself rushing by with no sign of slowing down.

In fact, Dave has been publishing cartoons nearly as long as I've been a Senator. He published his first cartoon in Ware, Massachusetts, in 1961, when I was a Suffolk County assistant district attorney after my brother's 1960 presidential campaign. By 1968, Dave's work was being published daily, and he's been a featured cartoonist of MetroWest Daily News in Framingham for 28 years. I typically hold my breath over breakfast in case he doesn't like something I just said or did, but that's thankfully rare, and I relax and laugh out loud at the day's fare.

Over the years, Dave has used his extraordinary talents to make us think, laugh and feel. He can praise or skewer us locally – from the emotional roller coaster of the Red Sox to the latest controversy in the Commonwealth we love. But he's a genius too in stirring images and humor on the great issues of the times – such as terrorism, the war in Iraq, and the world's response to the tsunami disaster in Indonesia. The ongoing changes in our country and world and the best and worst in our humanity are captured daily by Dave, and he's endlessly inspiring with his insights and hilarious depictions.

After the tragic attacks of 9-11, it took time before America could laugh again. Dave walked that line well, and his moving images helped ease us back from the void to a place where we could laugh again and look forward with hope and new confidence. No one does it better.

— *Sen. Edward M. Kennedy*

Introduction

Editorial page editors aren't known for their modesty. After all, we unblushingly force our considered opinions on thousands of readers every day. We presume to speak for the newspaper organizations of which we are really only a small part. We tell legislatures how to write laws and people how to vote. We're not a self-effacing bunch.

We are kept humble, however, by politicians and voters who stubbornly refuse to follow our advice, not to mention by readers who daily point out the error in our ways.

There's another thing that keeps this editorial page editor humble: having my work appear on the same page as Dave Granlund's cartoons.

Dave's fans regularly put me in my place. I'll write an editorial that cuts through a tricky issue like a precision laser, that scales new heights of rhetoric, elevating the public discourse while eviscerating those who disagree with me. But what will draw the impassioned letters? What will end up clipped from the page and posted on bulletin boards? What will be the talk of the newsroom and the company cafeteria? Dave's cartoon.

Often that cartoon will underline the editorial next to it, always bringing more humor and more bite to the issue at hand than I can muster with mere words. The editorial will often reflect Dave's thoughts as well, if only because we talk every day about whatever's in the news. In the decade I've been running the opinion pages of the MetroWest Daily News, he has been my most valued collaborator.

It's quite rare for a newspaper our size to have a full-time editorial cartoonist on site. Decades of newspaper consolidation and downsizing have thinned the ranks of cartoonists. It's so much cheaper to purchase syndicated cartoons for a few bucks a shot. What those newspapers miss is the local perspective Dave brings to his work every day. His cartoons don't just target national figures, they illustrate the life of a region we call home. He can zing a local politician one day, encapsulate a national issue the next, then turn his focus to the mosquitoes that are disrupting MetroWest barbecues.

The MetroWest Daily News has faced the same pressures as others in our industry. I'd like to say we kept Dave on the job because we are more steadfast in our local focus and devoted to editorial excellence. We are, of course, but there's a more important reason for Dave's longevity: If we let him go, our readers would never forgive us. There is simply no staff member more popular in the towns of MetroWest and more closely identified with the MetroWest Daily News.

The wall of Dave's office features prominently a large, framed print of a Thomas Nast cartoon. He sees himself as part of that grand tradition of editorial cartooning. He uses the old tools – india ink, seasonal references and the symbolic language cartoonists have always used to represent ideas.

Dave does something else that could be regarded as old-fashioned: He draws caricatures that actually look like the people he is portraying. This has become something of a lost art in modern cartooning. Cartoonists today seem content to let a few broad strokes represent a public figure; some keep recognizable figures out of the frame or replace them with a symbol, mainly because they are incapable of drawing real people.

Not Dave. He studies faces and keeps files on prominent people he might draw. He draws realistic portraits as well as caricatures. He knows how faces change to reflect different emotions. In his cartoons, the faces of famous people tell us things words alone cannot convey.

I could provide an analysis of Dave Granlund's artistry that cuts like a precision laser, scales new rhetorical heights and elevates the public discourse on editorial cartooning, but I know you're about to turn the page. Dave's cartoons will outshine my words again. So go ahead. Enjoy the best our opinion pages have to offer.

— Rick Holmes
Opinion Editor
MetroWest Daily News
July 12, 2005

Why the tunnel project is called the "BIG DIG"...

Where to find Osama bin Laden...

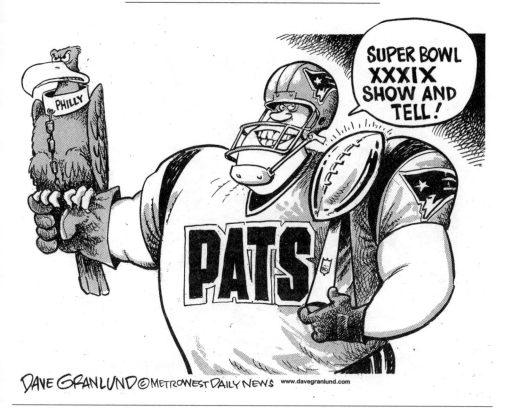

School lunch diet according to USDA...

When juveniles are charged as adults...

TREND : DOLLS TO LOOK MORE LIKE REGULAR PEOPLE...

Tribute to Mother Teresa

NEWS ITEM: LLOYDS OF LONDON SUFFERS BIGGEST LOSS IN 304 YEARS.

DAVE GRANLUND© www.davegranlund.com

DAVE GRANLUND©METROWEST DAILY NEWS.
www.davegranlund.com

SERB BODY ARMOR...

DAVE GRANLUND © 2000 METROWEST DAILY NEWS.

LONGEST DAY'S KNIGHT MEETS HARD DAY'S KNIGHT...

SIR WINSTON CHURCHILL

SIR PAUL McCARTNEY

DAVE GRANLUND © 1997 MIDDLESEX NEWS.

DAVE GRANLUND © 2000 METROWEST DAILY NEWS.

DAVE GRANLUND © METROWEST DAILY NEWS www.davegranlund.com

SCHOOL NUTRITION PROGRAM   SCHOOL EXERCISE PROGRAM

PROPOSAL: ALLOW ADS ON POLICE CRUISERS...

Pearl Harbor tribute

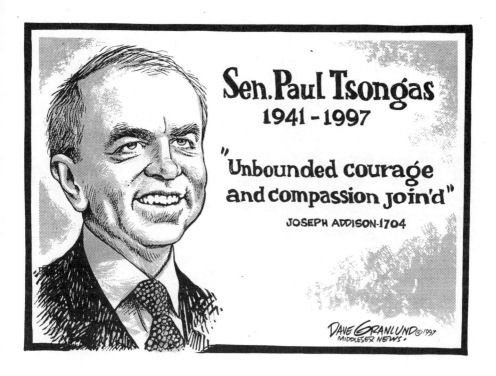

CLINTONS BEGIN VINEYARD VACATION...

The only debating Ted does these days...

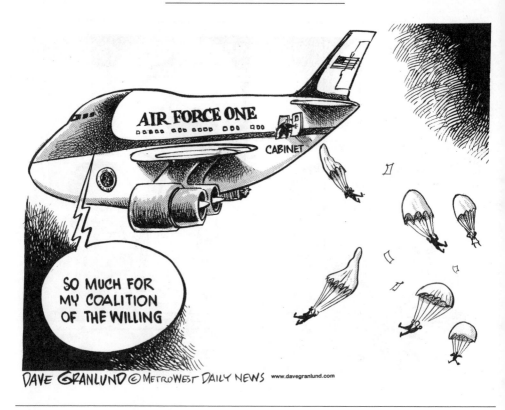

GEORGE BUSH

Kennebunkport, Maine

June 25, 1994

Dear Dave,

We just returned from a cruise to the Greek Isles accompanied by 11 grand children and other family. The kids behaved well, but I needed a relaxed laugh when we got back. And, lo and behold, here on my desk were those great cartoons. Thanks so very much for giving them to me.

Long after I am looking down, hopefully from above, these cartoons will grace our Presidential Library at Texas A&M, giving students and scholars a glimpse of what decent cartoon humor is all about.

Your Dad is just two days younger than I am. He sounds like my kind of guy; so give him a warm abrazo, and tell him, though his son's daggers did indeed come my way, they never clipped me below the belt. Even the negative ones were outweighed by some very positive ones.(My favorite? The "Rather" one of course).

We enjoyed our short visit to Petersham - such a lovely corner of the State in which I was born. Many, many thanks for this present that I will cherish.

Sincerely,

George Bush

PS pardon my home typing

BBP

May 23rd 1997
Walker's Point
Kennebunkport, Maine 04046

Dear Dave Granlund —

How kind of you to send
us the marvelous 1994 cartoon
of Millie. She was a great dog
and we absolutely adored her!
she is where she ought to be...
with the other angels!

again — george and I both
thank you for your note, the
cartoon and the others —

Warmly —

Barbara Bush

The cartoon will end in george's
library in Texas at College
Station —

The only member of the Bush family not running
for office...

GRANLUND © 1994 MIDDLESEX NEWS

CHARLES REMARRIES ...

DAVE GRANLUND © METROWEST DAILY NEWS   www.davegranlund.com

DAVE GRANLUND©
www.davegranlund.com

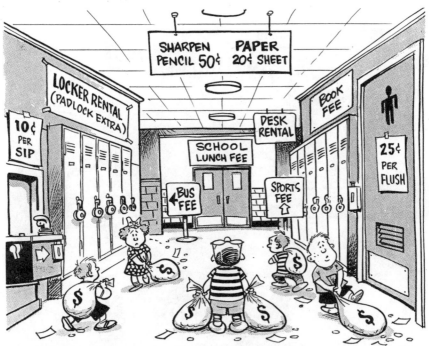

Guess which one has a higher batting average?

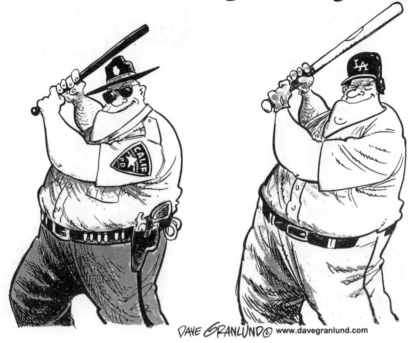

ITEM: MORE UNEMPLOYED EXECS USING FOOD PANTRIES...

DEFINITION OF **OUTPATIENT** TREATMENT...

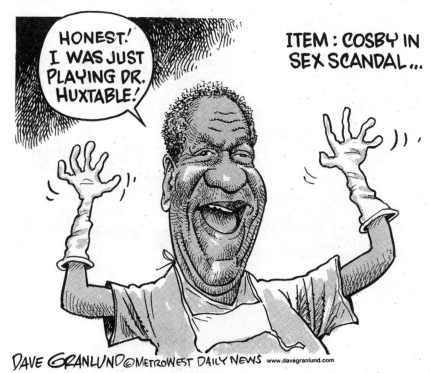

Victory over Japan anniversary

REPORT: OBESITY ON THE RISE...

U.S. TROOP ROTATION PLAN...

Guess which one was grabbed more quickly at the RI night club inferno?

DAVE GRANLUND ©METROWEST DAILY NEWS www.davegranlund.com

DAVE GRANLUND ©METROWEST DAILY NEWS www.davegranlund.com

DAVE GRANLUND © METROWEST DAILY NEWS   www.davegranlund.com

DAVE GRANLUND © METROWEST DAILY NEWS · www.davegranlund.com

NEWS ITEM: KKK WANTS TO SPONSOR ADOPT-A-HIGHWAY PROGRAM IN FLA.

DAVE GRANLUND © 1997 MIDDLESEX NEWS.

DAVE GRANLUND © 1999 METROWEST DAILY NEWS

ITEM: NEW ENGLAND COYOTES BECOMING MORE BOLD...

SEND OUT FLUFFY!

DAVE GRANLUND © METROWEST DAILY NEWS
www.davegranlund.com

Item: Jackson says he needs rest after trial...

The Bay State's idea of having a roof over your head...

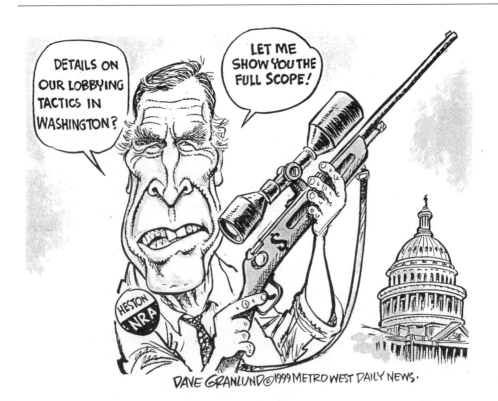

Item: BAA has plan to keep marathoners off lawns...

Pike tolls yet to come...

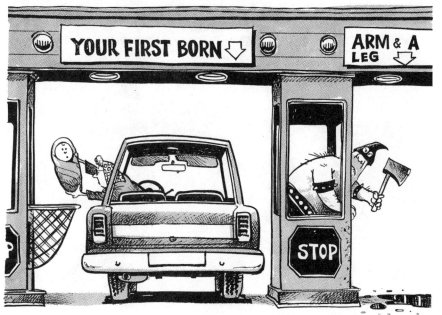

YOUR FIRST BORN ⬇

ARM & A LEG ⬇

STOP

DAVE GRANLUND ©2009 METROWEST DAILY NEWS

DAVE GRANLUND©
METROWEST DAILY NEWS
www.davegranlund.com

WEST BANK

CONSTRUCTION

SHARON

GW

U.S. OPPOSITION

New England
WINTER ATTIRE

New England
SPRING ATTIRE

DAVE GRANLUND© METROWEST DAILY NEWS
www.davegranlund.com

THE CAPITOL HONOR GUARD
of SOUTH CAROLINA

DAVE GRANLUND©2000METROWEST DAILY NEWS

Note: this is the one cartoon I regretted drawing –
many took offense to Iwo Jima style pose.

Tribute to JFK

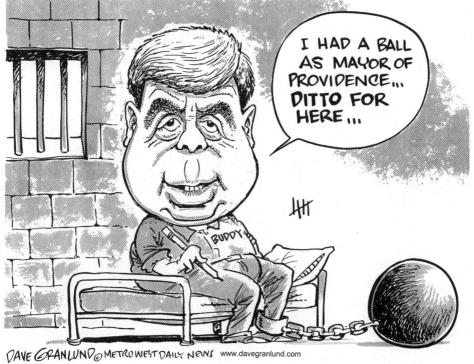

ITEM: McDonald's SUFFERS 1st QUARTERLY LOSS EVER...

DAVE GRANLUND © METROWEST DAILY NEWS

DAVE GRANLUND © METRO WEST DAILY NEWS
www.davegranlund.com

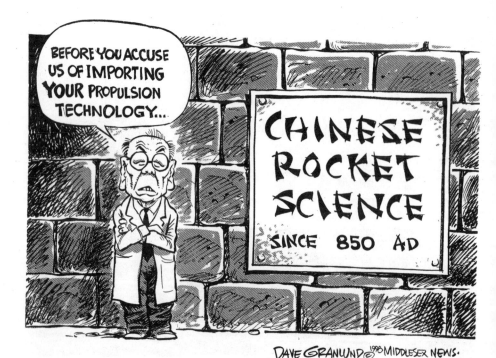

Looking For State Budget Surplus

Potty Shortage at Boston Marathon

2004 Democratic National Convention in Boston

Solution to Crowed Links

Annual Holiday display Tug-O-War

Operation *Desert Swarm* – Media Imbedded with Troops in Iraq

Iraq's First Steps Toward Democracy

Faces of 2003

Bush & Kerry Debates in 2004

Politics and the Press

The Blame Game

Patriots fans vs. the Boston mayor and police

Michael Jackson walks

Baghdad Christmas

Bush Set to Topple Saddam

Would Massachusetts be ready for a Tsunami

DAVE GRANLUND ·08

What the BIG DIG Really Digs

Government video games to recruit young minds

Dave Granlund ©
MetroWest Daily News

Hindsight and Wars

What Replaces Paper Ballots

Marriage in the New Millennium

The Super-sizing of America

Beaver Trapping Curbed in Bay State

Missile Defense Test Fails

New England Weather

Mixed Signals From U.S. Immigration

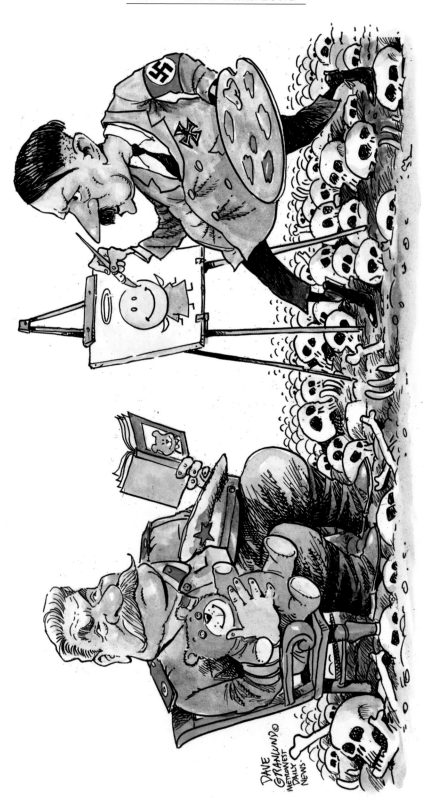

Report: Stalin and Hitler had Softer Sides

DAVE GRANLUND © MetroWest Daily News

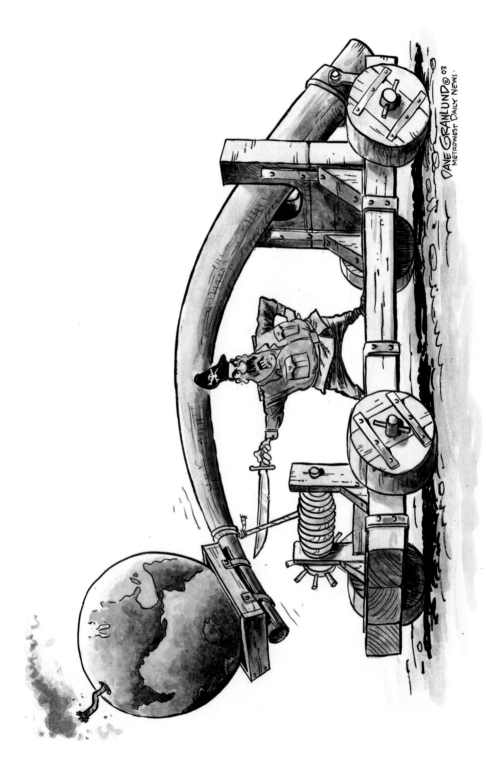

Saddam's 2003 Sabre Rattling

2004 Highlights

Report: Mass. Couples Stay Married Longest in U.S.

Gov. Romney Tries to Storm Beacon Hill

2004 Republican National Convention in New York

Mall Crawl Gridlock

Nation Building

60 Minutes...

60 Seconds...

POLICE ROAD DETAIL HAND SIGNALS...

Dave Granlund ©2000 MetroWest Daily News.

HOWARD STERN SUSPENDED UNTIL HE CLEANS UP ACT...

Dave Granlund © MetroWest Daily News
www.davegranlund.com

1961...ROGER MARIS POPS ANOTHER FOR A HOME RUN...

1998...MARK McGWIRE POPS ANOTHER FOR A HOME RUN...

DAVE GRANLUND © 1998 MIDDLESEX NEWS.

ER... NO, THAT'S JUST FOR GAS...

SALE!

$450.00 PER MONTH

DAVE GRANLUND © METROWEST DAILY NEWS   www.davegranlund.com

ITEM : STATEWIDE SMOKING BAN WOULD EXEMPT NURSING HOMES

How to solve the salmonella problem...

DAVE GRANLUND ©1995 MIDDLESEX NEWS·

DAVE GRANLUND ©1996 MIDDLESEX NEWS·

Spin Doctors...

Inspiration for US electric power grid...

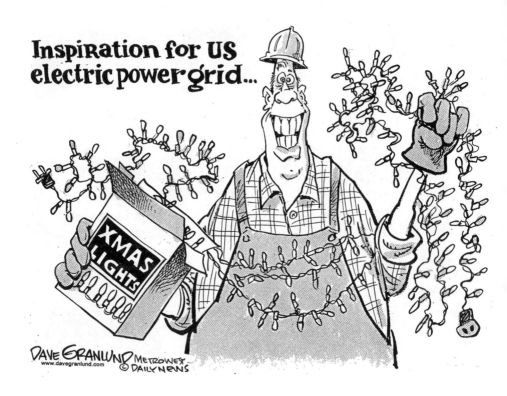

Item: N.E. has highest illegal drug use in U.S.

ITEM: BARRY BONDS ON CRUTCHES; MAY MISS SEASON...

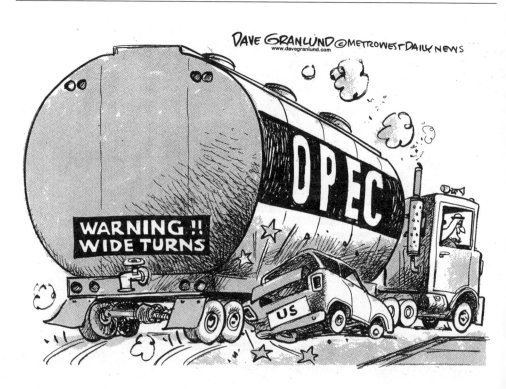

Item: Mick Jagger to be Knighted by Queen ...

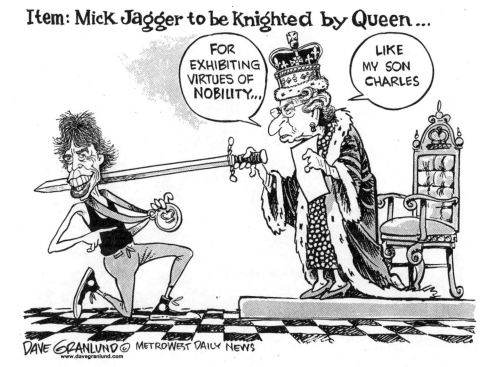

Dave Granlund © MetroWest Daily News.
www.davegranlund.com

Refresher course for New England meteorologists...

Dave Granlund © MetroWest Daily News
www.davegranlund.com

ITEM: CRUISE LINE VIRUS SPREADS TO DISNEY SHIP...

HIKER HATS NOT TO WEAR DURING BAY STATE HUNTING SEASON...

Clues that your local beach may have problems...

RAP GROUP CHAUFFEUR...

DAVE GRANLUND ©2000 METROWEST DAILY NEWS.

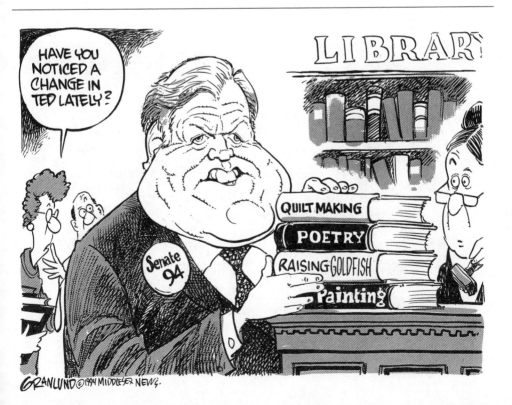

News item : Shuttle Columbia has plumbing problems...

ITEM: MARTHA STEWART GOES TO PRISON...

MAINE TOURIST BOARD'S ANSWER TO ICE STORMS

White House insists 9-11 panel question Bush & Cheney jointly...

NEWS ITEM: OSCAR NOMINEES ANNOUNCED...

New Hampshire's Old Man of Mountain falls

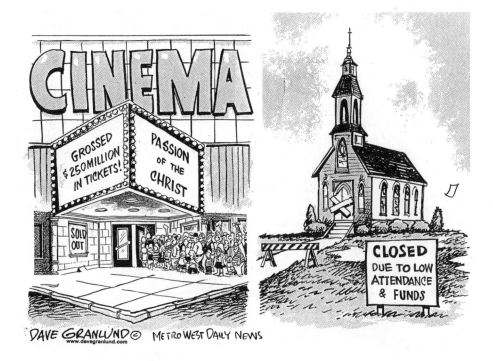

DAVE GRANLUND© 1995 MIDDLESEX NEWS.

DAVE GRANLUND © 1999 METROWEST DAILY NEWS.

The difference between a playoff ref and a Super Bowl ref ...

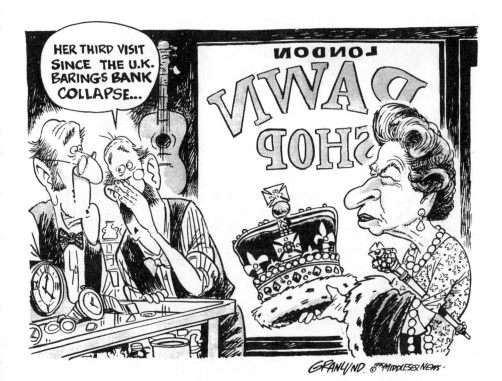

NEWS ITEM: WORCESTER POLICE SHOOT BEAR...

ITEM: CASTRO MARKS 45 YEARS IN POWER...

DAVE GRANLUND © MetroWest Daily News.
www.davegranlund.com

DAVE GRANLUND © MetroWest Daily News   www.davegranlund.com

Tribute to John F. Kennedy Jr.

Item : 66-year-old woman gives birth...

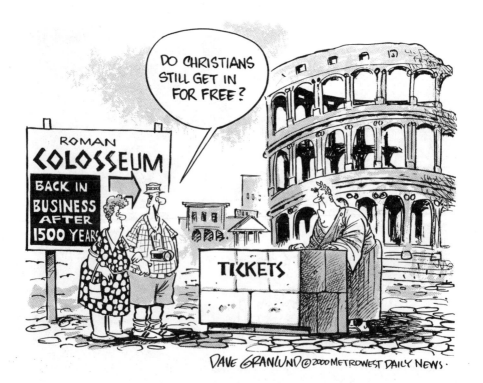

New England snowstorm indicators...

LIGHT   MODERATE   NOR'EASTER

DAVE GRANLUND © METRO WEST DAILY NEWS ·
www.davegranlund.com

GRANLUND 1991 © MIDDLESEX NEWS ·

HEALTH CARE COSTS

Bay Staters prepare for hunting season ...

... One snake that St. Patrick missed...

Veteran's Day Tribute to my father Earl Granlund, USMC

The emperor's new clothes...

WHAT LOGAN SECURITY HAS BEEN BEST AT PROTECTING...

Gore's last stand...

NEWS ITEM: BOSTON MARATHON TO HAVE TIGHTER SECURITY...

NEWS ITEM: FRANCE CATCHES 5 AMERICAN SPIES.

ITEM: POSTAL SERVICE MAY OPT FOR OVERHAUL

DAVE GRANLUND © METROWEST DAILY NEWS   www.davegranlund.com

GRANLUND © 1994 MIDDLESEX NEWS·